Feeling Scared

For a free color catalog describing Gareth Stevens' list of high-quality books and multimedia programs, call 1-800-542-2595 (USA) or 1-800-461-9120 (Canada). Gareth Stevens Publishing's Fax: (414) 225-0377. See our catalog, too, on the World Wide Web: http://gsinc.com

The author and original publisher would like to thank the staff and pupils of the following schools for their help in the making of this book: St. Vincent de Paul Roman Catholic School, Westminster; Mayfield Primary School, Cambridge; Swavesey Village College, Cambridge.

Library of Congress Cataloging-in-Publication Data

Althea.
    Feeling scared / by Althea Braithwaite; photographs by Charlie Best; illustrations by Conny Jude.
       p. cm. — (Exploring emotions)
    Includes bibliographical references and index.
    Summary: Examines the nature of fear, its different kinds, how it can be sensible or fun, and how it can be controlled.
    ISBN 0-8368-2118-1 (lib. bdg.)
    1. Fear in children—Juvenile literature. [1. Fear.] I. Best, Charlie, ill. II. Jude, Conny, ill. III. Title. IV. Series: Althea. Exploring emotions.
BF723.F4A724 1998
152.4'6—dc21   98-5586

This North American edition first published in 1998 by
Gareth Stevens Publishing
1555 North RiverCenter Drive, Suite 201
Milwaukee, Wisconsin 53212 USA

This U.S. edition © 1998 by Gareth Stevens, Inc.
First published in 1997 by A & C Black (Publishers) Limited, 35 Bedford Row, London WC1R 4JH. Text © 1997 by Althea Braithwaite. Photographs © 1997 by Charlie Best. Illustrations © 1997 by Conny Jude. Additional end matter © 1998 by Gareth Stevens, Inc.

Series consultant: Dr. Dorothy Rowe

Gareth Stevens series editor: Dorothy L. Gibbs
Editorial assistant: Diane Laska

Printed in Mexico

1 2 3 4 5 6 7 8 9 02 01 00 99 98

Feeling Scared

Althea

Photographs by
Charlie Best

Illustrations by
Conny Jude

Gareth Stevens Publishing
MILWAUKEE

Shona says, "At night, when I hear noises, I think people are coming to get me. I know that's silly, but I can't help it!"

I'm afraid of storms. I hate thunder, and I'm sure I'll be struck by lightning.

What scares you?

5

Different people react to fear in different ways. Some people feel like running away or just sinking into the ground.

I get cold and shivery.

My stomach churns, and I feel queasy.

6

Most people have been scared of the dark at one time or another. Things can seem much scarier at night — you can feel very alone. Noises seem much louder when it's quiet.

"I kept having the same nightmare every night, and I was afraid to go to sleep. I didn't tell my mom. I just said I wasn't tired and didn't want to go to bed."

Sam remembers, "I was afraid to be upstairs alone. I used to try to get my brother to come up and play on his computer, so someone else would be upstairs with me."

When I wake up at night, I'm frightened by the strange shadows on the walls.

The dreams we have at night are jumbles of ideas, experiences, and feelings we have hidden during the day. If you felt very angry, but didn't show it, that anger might become a frightening monster in your dream. But dreaming about something doesn't make it happen.

Not everything that worries us makes us feel scared. Sometimes we just feel a little nervous or uneasy.

Jan says, "I'm nervous when I plan to stay overnight with a friend. It's silly of me, because I always enjoy myself when I'm actually there."

I went fishing at the pond and fell in. I was scared because I can't swim, and my boots were filling up with water.

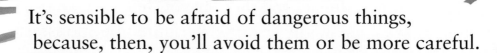

It's sensible to be afraid of dangerous things, because, then, you'll avoid them or be more careful.

People who say they're never frightened are more likely to take risks that could be dangerous.

Danny's always taking chances on his bike. He's nearly been knocked off twice this year already.

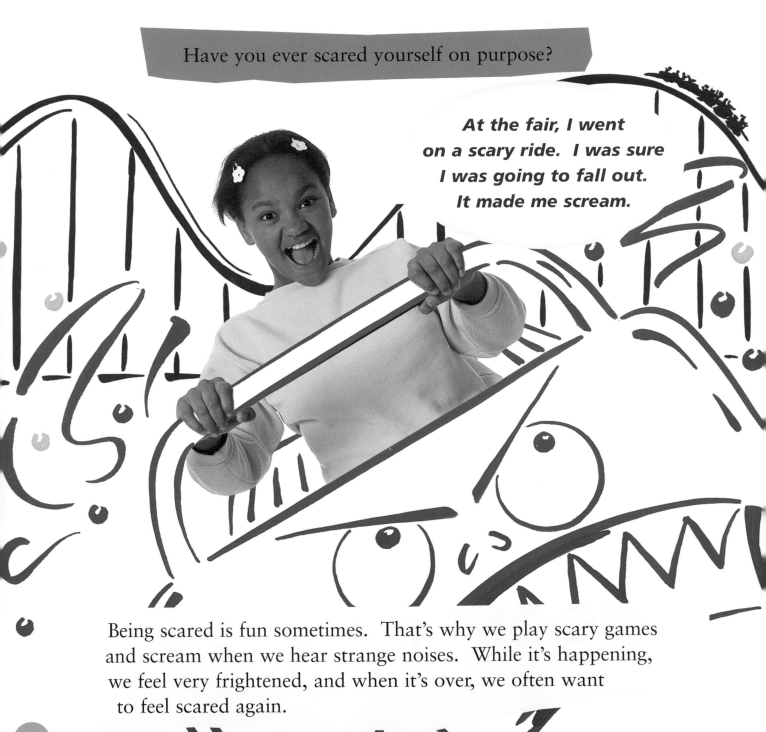

Have you ever scared yourself on purpose?

*At the fair, I went
on a scary ride. I was sure
I was going to fall out.
It made me scream.*

Being scared is fun sometimes. That's why we play scary games and scream when we hear strange noises. While it's happening, we feel very frightened, and when it's over, we often want to feel scared again.

It's all right to want the thrills of being scared when you know everything will be fine. If you end up too frightened, however, you might not be able to stop being scared just by telling yourself to stop.

When I'm reading an exciting ghost story, I get scared, but I can't stop reading it.

New situations can sometimes be scary. When we don't know what's going to happen next, we're not sure how to behave.

Shona says, "When someone I don't even know is mean to me, I get scared, and I start thinking the whole world is a dangerous place."

"I get scared when I have to answer the phone. I don't know who it will be or if I'll know what to say."

Ring Ring

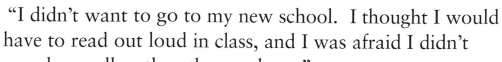
"I didn't want to go to my new school. I thought I would have to read out loud in class, and I was afraid I didn't read as well as the other students."

Sometimes, even when you're scared stiff, it's difficult to admit it to close friends or to your parents. Often, however, when you finally tell them what's scaring you, you discover that they feel the same way.

Many people feel frightened by things they can't control.

When my parents have an argument, I'm afraid Dad will leave us, like my friend's dad did.

When my mom gets sick, I'm scared she might die.

It doesn't help when someone says, "Don't worry, it won't happen." We all know bad things do happen, but we can't stop them from happening by worrying about them.

It does help to enjoy the present and stop worrying about things that are out of your control. You can try to stop yourself from dwelling on worries by saying, "I'm not going to think about that right now." It might also help to think about something nice or to tell yourself a story to take your mind off whatever is frightening you.

It's easy to be afraid that something awful is going to happen when you don't know all the facts about a situation.

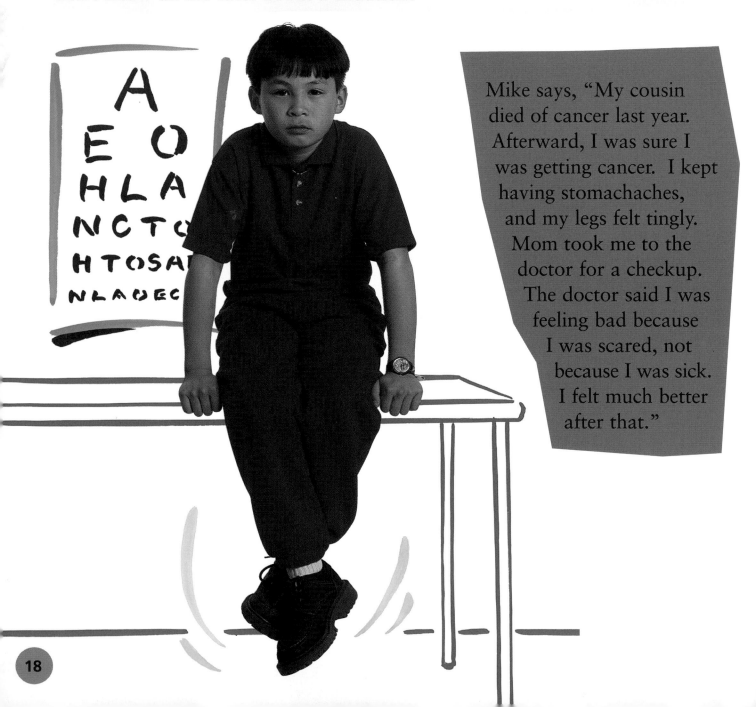

Mike says, "My cousin died of cancer last year. Afterward, I was sure I was getting cancer. I kept having stomachaches, and my legs felt tingly. Mom took me to the doctor for a checkup. The doctor said I was feeling bad because I was scared, not because I was sick. I felt much better after that."

My friend has a skin problem, called eczema, and I thought I would get it, too, because I used her towel. Then she told me eczema isn't catching.

When you're scared of something, and you don't know all the facts, it's a good idea to ask questions. You might be frightened over nothing.

19

There are lots of ways to keep from being scared.

When I'm in bed, I shut my eyes and tell myself there's nothing to be afraid of. Then I think of something nice, like my birthday party.

Sam says, "I watched a spooky video, over and over again, until it didn't scare me anymore."

"When there's a storm, I close the curtains, and I turn up the TV to drown out most of the thunder."

What do you do to keep from being scared?

Over time, most of us learn to cope with many different fears. After dealing with a scary experience once, it might not be so frightening the next time.

"I was scared when I was learning to ride a bike, and I felt silly every time I fell off. I thought I would never be able to do it, but, after a while, I got the hang of it. Now it doesn't seem scary at all!"

"When I fell and cut my knee on some glass, I was afraid I would need stitches. At the hospital, I did have stitches, but it wasn't so bad."

"When I was younger, I was afraid of escalators. I thought I might get caught at the top and be sucked in. I know that won't happen — but I still jump off fast when I get to the top!"

When you talk about your fears with other people, you will find that they have fears, too.

Sometimes I'm just scared without knowing why.

We all have unexplained fears at times. Even your heroes, the people you admire most, sometimes feel frightened. You can't be courageous or brave if you never feel frightened.

When you're afraid of something but overcome your fear, you are braver than someone who is not afraid.

For Teachers and Parents
A Note from Dorothy Rowe

Children often feel frightened. Unfortunately, adults frequently belittle or ignore a child's fears. Sometimes, the adult thinks the child's fears are not important; sometimes the adult also is frightened but doesn't want to admit it. To help a child deal with fear, adults must keep in mind that fear arises from how people interpret situations, so they must make an effort to find out how the child is interpreting his or her situation.

A child won't see a situation the same way an adult does for the simple reason that no two people, whatever their ages, ever see things in exactly the same way. A child, for instance, might not interpret a one in a million chance of getting cancer as good odds for staying well, whereas some adults think that one in fourteen million are good odds for winning the lottery!

The seemingly irrational fears of children, like fear of the dark, usually relate to major issues we all face — dying, losing someone we love, meeting people who might be hostile. Many people, not just children, are scared of the dark or of being at home alone, but they often won't admit it because they're afraid their fear sounds silly. One person admitting to a fear, however, seems to make it much easier for others to admit their fears.

Adults must be prepared to tell children what frightens them and what they have tried to do to overcome their fears, but they should not pretend to provide easy solutions. This way, adults and children can work out practical ways to deal with fear together, and children can develop a philosophy of life that recognizes the importance of courage.

Suggestions for Discussions

To start a discussion and get everyone involved, you and the children could write lists of all the things that make you feel scared. Then, compare lists. Encourage the children to discuss the fears that some of them have but others don't, as well as the fears that many of them seem to have in common.

Many different fears and ways to cope with feeling scared can be discussed with children while going through this book, page by page. The following points might help start your discussions.

Page 5
Fear can come from not knowing enough about the things that scare us to realize that they are not as threatening as they might seem.

Page 8
Some children have been threatened that they are being watched from "above," and, if they don't behave, they will be punished, possibly in some unexpected way. To many of these children, this punishment seems more likely to happen in the dark.

Page 9
With a large group of children, it might take too long for each child to tell about his or her bad dreams or nightmares, but the children could write about them or draw pictures to illustrate them.

Pages 10-11
Some people need to be more aware of the danger of their actions. Those who are cautious should never be made to feel cowardly. Taking dares or playing in dangerous places can cause serious injuries or even death, as drownings and accidents on railroad tracks have proven.

Pages 12-13
Doing scary things on purpose might seem more exciting than frightening because you generally know what to expect and are able to prepare yourself. What happens, though, when a situation becomes scarier than you expected — possibly too scary?

Page 14
New situations are often very scary, but, with proper guidance and assistance, they can be excellent opportunities for learning. Children need help understanding new experiences. When they are not so confused about a situation, they usually are less frightened, too.

Page 15
Many children have fears that arise from a lack of self-confidence. Talking together and finding out that others feel the same way can often boost self-confidence.

Pages 16-17
Sadly, bad things happen sometimes, and people can be terrified about how they will survive if something bad happens to them. In spite of the great unhappiness and pain you might feel when someone you love leaves you or dies, you do manage to survive.

Pages 18-19
Sometimes adults need to learn all the facts, too, so they won't instill fears in children because of their own lack of information. Parents tend, also, to pass on their more general fears to their children. If, for example, they

consistently portray the world as a dangerous place where no one can be trusted, or they always worry about "what the neighbors will say," their children often pick up those same anxieties and might become fearful.

Page 20
Deciding not to do things that scare you doesn't make you a coward. In fact, frightening yourself needlessly seems a little foolish. Maybe the child should have decided not to watch the spooky video at all.

Page 22
Courage is the key to coping with many kinds of fear. Sometimes this means having the courage to look or feel a little silly, at first, in order to learn something new.

Page 24
We all have unexplained feelings of fear from time to time, but we must not let them overpower us or prevent us from doing things that are important or enjoyable.

More Books to Read

Alice the Brave. Phyllis R. Naylor (Simon and Schuster Trade)

Brave. Feelings (series). Janine Amos (Raintree Steck-Vaughn)

Brave Maddie Egg. Natalie Standiford (Random Books)

Emotional Ups and Downs. Good Health Guides (series). Enid Fisher (Gareth Stevens)

Herbie Jones and the Dark Attic. Suzy Kline (Puffin Books)

No Turning Back: Dillon Confronts Death on a Magic Journey. Beth Peterson (Simon and Schuster Children's)

When the Water Closes over My Head. Donna J. Napoli (Dutton Children's Books)

Videos to Watch

Everyone Gets Scared Sometimes. (Sunburst Communications)

I'm Feeling Scared. Feelings (series). (Churchill Media)

The Scary Sounds in the Campground. Quigley's Village (series). (Zondervan Publishing House)

A Time to Be Brave. (Beacon Films)

Web Sites to Visit

www.pbs.org/adventures/

www.roots.com/stories/stories.html

Due to the dynamic nature of the Internet, some web sites stay current longer than others. To find additional web sites, use a reliable search engine with one or more of the following keywords to help you locate information about feeling angry. Keywords: *anxiety, behavior, emotions, fear, feelings, fright, phobia.*

Glossary

cancer — a dangerous illness that occurs when groups of cells in the body grow irregularly into lumps, called tumors.

churn — to stir roughly with a beating or grinding motion; to agitate.

cope — to deal with, or overcome, a problem or a difficult situation.

courage — strength of mind and emotions to face danger, fears, or serious difficulties.

dangerous — possibly able to cause harm, loss, or injury.

drown out — to prevent sounds from being heard by making other sounds that are closer or louder.

dwell on — to give attention to for a long period of time.

eczema — a skin disease identified by redness, itching, and crusty sores.

escalator — a "belt" of power-driven, mechanical stairs that moves continuously up or down.

fright — fear that is caused by some unexpected danger or something very scary.

hang — skill gained after practice to do or understand something.

nervous — jumpy, uneasy, unsteady.

nightmare — a very scary dream — one that might wake you up.

queasy — feeling sick, upset, or unsettled in the stomach.

risk — a situation that could cause harm, loss, or injury.

sensible — having or using reason, awareness, or good judgement.

spooky — ghostlike or haunting.

worry — to be concerned, disturbed, or fearful about something.

Index

ML